TOPIARIES
&indoor trees
floral displays

TOPIARIES
& indoor trees
floral displays

stunning structures from flowers, foliage and fruit

southwater

This edition is published by Southwater

Southwater is an imprint of Anness Publishing Ltd
Hermes House, 88–89 Blackfriars Road, London SE1 8HA
tel. 020 7401 2077; fax 020 7633 9499
www.southwaterbooks.com; info@anness.com

© Anness Publishing Ltd 1997, 2003

UK agent: The Manning Partnership Ltd, 6 The Old Dairy, Melcombe Road, Bath BA2 3LR; tel. 01225 478 444; fax
01225 478 440; sales@manning-partnership.co.uk

UK distributor: Grantham Book Services Ltd, Isaac Newton Way, Alma Park Industrial Estate, Grantham, Lincs NG31
9SD; tel. 01476 541080; fax 01476 541061; orders@gbs.tbs-ltd.co.uk

North American agent/distributor: National Book Network, 4501 Forbes Boulevard, Suite 200, Lanham, MD 20706; tel.
301 459 3366; fax 301 429 5746; www.nbnbooks.com

Australian agent/distributor: Pan Macmillan Australia, Level 18, St Martins Tower, 31 Market St, Sydney, NSW 2000;
tel. 1300 135 113; fax 1300 135 103; customer.service@macmillan.com.au

A CIP catalogue record for this book is available from the British Library.

Publisher: Joanna Lorenz
Project Editor: Joanne Rippin
Designers: Lisa Tai and LIlian Lindblom
Illustrations: Anna Koska

Previously published as part of the *Gifts from Nature* series

1 3 5 7 9 10 8 6 4 2

Acknowledgements: thanks to the following project contributors:
Fiona Barnett pp 11, 16, 18, 24, 34, 36, 38, 52, 53, 60, 62; Kally Ellis and Ercole Moroni p 22;
Tessa Evelegh pp 13, 14, 20, 28, 54, 56; Gilly Love p 42; Terence Moore pp 12, 31, 32, 40, 41, 43-49, 58, 59;
Katherine Richmond p 17, 30; Pamela Westland p 10
Photographs by: James Duncan, John Freeman, Michelle Garrett, Debbie Patterson, Polly Wreford.

CONTENTS

INTRODUCTION

The elegance of formal gardening comes indoors in this collection of arrangements inspired by the clean geometric shapes of clipped topiary hedges and trees. Mop-head trees, 17th-century-style obelisks and elegant cones make sophisticated floral decorations for even the most restrained of room settings. In keeping with their formal style, topiary arrangements frequently look best when composed of a single type of material. A mass of lavender heads, a tightly packed sphere of dried roses or a symmetrical arrangement of silvery blue pine (spruce) are all simple to put together but very stylish, and have even more impact when arranged in pairs.

Dried flowers, foliage, fir cones, fruit – even seashells – all make long-lasting topiary arrangements, but you can use the same techniques to make fabulous fresh flower decorations, perfect for weddings and special celebrations. Choose scented flowers to give an extra dimension. Dried arrangements can be scented with essential oils or whole spices to add their delicious, lasting aromas.

Pomanders have been made for centuries to scent cupboards and drawers and to ward off bad odours. The traditional clove-studded orange, carefully dried, will go on smelling wonderful for ages. Its warm, spicy perfume, redolent of mulled wine, has become especially associated with Christmas, and decorative pomanders look lovely hanging on the tree or piled in a bowl. Scented balls of spices or flowers make delightful decorations all through the yearhanging from a kitchen dresser, or looped over a bedroom mirror.

Left: A traditional pomander decorated with golden ribbon and a gilt heart.

BALLS AND POMANDERS

The delicious, long-lasting scent of citrus pomanders has remained popular since medieval times. Both oranges and cloves were then rich and rare commodities, while sweet scents were  a necessary defence against the pungent smells of everyday life. Traditional pomanders, with their spicy, wintry combination of scents, still have the power to evoke a feeling of richness and luxury which

 makes them ideal Christmas decorations, bound with lengths of sumptuous velvet, satin or gold-shot ribbon. Flower and herb balls are another lovely way to scent and decorate a room.

MEDIEVAL POMANDERS

❧

Well-made pomanders will continue to smell wonderful for years. Hang them in wardrobes and cupboards to waft their warm, subtle perfume over your clothes. For more short-term decorations, stud the fruits with patterns of cloves, leaving some of the skin exposed.

- firm, unblemished citrus fruits
- 1 cm (½ in) wide tape
- scissors
- pins
- nail or darning needle
- whole cloves
- paper bag
- ground orris root
- 1 cm (½ in) wide ribbon

1 To make a traditional pomander, wrap a length of tape around an orange, criss-crossing it at the top and bottom of the fruit, to divide it into four segments. Pin the tape in place. Using a nail or darning needle to pierce the skin, push in whole cloves to outline each segment, then fill in the whole of each area of skin.

2 To make decorations to hang on the Christmas tree, use a selection of citrus fruits such as clementines, lemons, kumquats and limes. Use a nail or darning needle to pierce the skin, then stud the fruit with whole cloves. Make geometric or spiral patterns, or push in the cloves at random.

3 When you have completed your designs, put the fruit into a paper bag and sprinkle in 15 ml (1 tbsp) ground orris root for each large fruit. Close the bag and leave in a warm place such as an airing cupboard for 2–3 weeks while the fruit dries and the spices mellow. Remove the tapes and replace them with decorative ribbons.

CHRISTMAS POMANDERS

Traditional pomanders have a warm spicy smell that suits the festive season perfectly. If you are making them at the last minute before Christmas there won't be time to dry them out. Arrange them in a bowl and turn them frequently so that they have a chance to dry in the warmth of the room: they'll still smell wonderful.

- 3 small, firm oranges
- 3 contrasting lengths of ribbon
- nail or darning needle
- cloves
- scissors

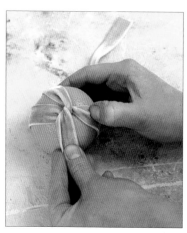

1 Tie a length of ribbon around each orange as if you were tying it around a parcel. Cross it over at the base and bring the ends up to the top of the orange.

2 Finish off by tying the ribbon into a bow. Adjust the position of the ribbon as necessary to ensure that the orange is divided into four equal-sized sections.

3 Starting at the edges of the sections, pierce the orange skin with a nail or darning needle and push in the cloves. Continue until each quarter is completely covered. Trim the ends of the ribbon neatly.

HANGING FLOWER BALLS

❧

A fragrant mixture of dried flowers in toning colours makes a charming hanging decoration. Handle the flowerheads as little as possible while you are making the ball. If you prefer, you could support it on a stem or trunk until it is almost complete, then just fill in the hole at the end.

- 9 cm (3½ in) diameter florist's dry foam ball
- stub (floral) wires
- assorted dried flowers such as achillea, ambrosinia, larkspur, marjoram, *Nigella orientalis*, oregano, roses
- 45 cm (18 in) ribbon
- scissors

1 Fix the hanging wire, for threading the ribbon, through the florist's dry foam ball before you begin to add any flowers. Bend a long stub (floral) wire in half like a large staple and push both long ends right through the centre of the ball.

2 Leave about 2.5 cm (1 in) of the looped wire sticking above the surface of the ball (this forms the loop that you will thread the ribbon through). Twist the two ends of the stub (floral) wire together under the ball.

3 Wire together bunches of three to four flowerheads, cutting all the stems to the same length. Insert them in the foam, keeping the design as balanced as possible and turning the ball gently as you work. Trim the completed ball lavishly with ribbon tied at the top and finished with a bow.

MARJORAM URN

Marjoram is one of the best dried herbs for decorative purposes, as it retains its green-tinged soft pink tones.
Teamed with a classic rust-coloured urn, it makes a charming table decoration.

- dried marjoram
- scissors
- 7.5 cm (3 in) diameter florist's dry foam ball
- 7.5 cm (3 in) diameter urn

1 Marjoram comes in a large, somewhat wild bunch, so start by snipping off the individual florets, leaving about 1 cm (½ in) for fixing into the florist's foam ball.

2 Make a ring of marjoram around the middle of the florist's foam ball then, working in circles, gradually fill until one half of the ball is covered.

3 Work a few more circles around the lower half of the ball. Put the ball in the urn, then fill in with more marjoram until the ball is totally covered.

LAVENDER POMANDER

This delightful lavender ball makes an aromatic and long-lasting room decoration for any time of the year.

- stub (floral) wire
- 9 cm (3½ in) diameter florist's dry foam ball
- 45 cm (18 in)
- ribbon
- wire cutters
- large bunch dried lavender stems
- scissors

1 Bend the wire in half and push it through the centre of the ball. Thread the ribbon through the wire loop and push it down to hold the ribbon firmly. Trim the wire ends and bend them against the foam to secure.

2 Trim all the lavender stems to about 3 cm (1¼ in). Select flowerheads of a similar size and, starting at the bottom of the foam ball, push the stems in, making a circle around the circumference of the ball.

3 When the first circle is complete, make another circle of lavender around the circumference at right angles to the first. This will divide the pomander into quarters.

4 Working in lines of lavender heads, fill in each quarter of the foam ball until it is completely and evenly covered. Tie a bow at the top of the ribbon for hanging.

ROSE AND CLOVE POMANDER

This pomander is a decadent display of rose heads massed in a ball. But it has a secret: cloves hidden between the rose heads give the pomander its lasting spicy perfume. You will need a large number of roses, but the pomander is simple to make and would be a very special gift.

- stub (floral) wire
- 10 cm (4 in) diameter florist's dry foam ball
- 45 cm (18 in) ribbon, 2.5 cm (1 in) wide

- wire cutters
- scissors
- 100 stems dried roses
- 25 g (1 oz) cloves

1 Bend the wire in half and push it through the centre of the ball. Thread the ribbon through the wire loop and push it down to hold the ribbon firmly. Trim the wire ends and bend them against the foam to secure.

2 Cut the stems of the dried roses to approximately 2.5 cm (1 in). Starting at the top of the foam ball, push the stems in to form a tightly packed ring around the ribbon loop. As you work, push a clove into the foam between each pair of roses. Continue to form concentric circles around the ball until it is completely covered.

ROSE AND CARDAMOM POMANDER

Fragrant cardamoms have an elegant shape that echoes that of small, pointed rosebuds, while their subtle green colour is an attractive foil for the soft pink flowers. When the colour of this delicate pomander has faded, spray it gold to make a Christmas ornament.

- 60 cm (24 in) ribbon or cord
- stub wire
- 7.5 cm (3 in) diameter florist's dry foam ball

- wire cutters
- scissors
- small rosebuds
- all-purpose glue
- green cardamom pods

1 Make a long loop with the ribbon or cord. Bind the base of the loop with wire, leaving a long end. Push this through the centre of the foam ball and out through the other side. Trim the wire to about 2.5 cm (1 in) and bend the end against the foam to secure.

2 Trim the stems of the rosebuds to approximately 2.5 cm (1 in) and push them into the foam to cover it completely. Use a little glue to secure the buds if the stems are very short. Once the foam is covered, glue green cardamom pods between the rosebuds to give a contrast in colour and texture.

DRIED POMANDER

This pomander is designed more for its visual impact than its scent. Little bridesmaids will find it easier to carry than a posy, or you could make it any time as a decoration for a bedroom – perhaps for the dressing-table – scenting it with potpourri oil.

- scissors
- 10 stems glycerined eucalyptus
- 15 cm (6 in) diameter florist's dry foam ball
- 45 cm (18 in) ribbon, 3 cm (1¼ in) wide

- stub (floral) wires
- 30 stems dried roses
- florist's reel wire
- florist's (stem-wrap) tape
- 12 stems dried pale pink peonies
- 12 dried apple slices
- 1 dried ti tree

1 Cut the eucalyptus stems into 10 cm (4 in) lengths. Make sure that the stem ends are clean and sharp, and carefully push them into the florist's foam ball, distributing them evenly over its surface.

2 To make a carrying handle, loop the ribbon in half and bind the two cut ends with a stub (floral) wire. Push the ends of the wire through the centre of the ball and bend them over at the other side to secure the ribbon.

3 Cut the stems of the roses to 4 cm (1½ in) and wire individually with stub (floral) wires. Bind them in groups of three using florist's reel wire and tape. Cut the peony stems to 4 cm (1½ in) and wire and tape them individually. Wire the dried apple slices individually.

4 Push the wired peonies into the foam ball, distributing them evenly. Do the same with the wired apple slices.

5 Distribute the groups of roses evenly over the ball. Cut the ti tree stems into 9 cm (3½ in) lengths and push into the foam to fill any remaining gaps. Once the ball is complete, reposition individual elements if necessary to create the best effect.

SPICED POMANDER

Based on the quartered design of the traditional orange pomander, this one makes a refreshing change with the sweet scent of cardamom and soft muted colours.

- cloves
- 7.5 cm (3 in) diameter florist's dry foam ball
- glue gun
- green cardamom pods
- natural raffia
- stub (floral) wire

1 Start by making a single line of cloves all around the circumference of the foam ball. Make another line at right angles to it to divide the ball into quarters.

2 Push in a line of cloves on each side of the original lines, to make broad bands of cloves quartering the foam ball.

3 Starting at the top of one quarter, glue cardamom pods to the foam, methodically working in rows to create an orderly effect. Repeat on the other three quarters.

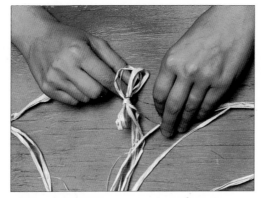

4 Put two or three strands of natural raffia together and tie a bow in the centre of the length. Pass a stub (floral) wire through the knot and twist the ends of the wire together.

5 Fix the bow to the top of the ball using the stub (floral) wire. Tie the loose ends of the raffia in a knot for hanging the pomander.

BRIDESMAID'S POMANDER

Popular in Victorian times, sweet-smelling pomanders make a pretty accessory for bridesmaids, and are easy for small children to carry as long as you remember to make the ribbon handle quite short.

- stub (floral) wires
- 9 cm (3½ in) diameter florist's dry foam ball
- red ribbon
- scissors
- dried red roses
- glue gun
- glycerined eucalyptus stems

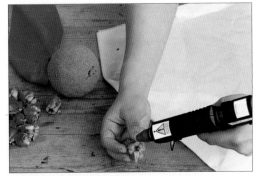

1 Bend a stub (floral) wire in half and push the ends through the centre of the foam ball, leaving a small loop. Bend the ends of the wire back into the ball. Tie the ribbon through the wire loop. Remove the rose heads from their stems and glue each of them to the ball using a glue gun.

2 Make a circle of rose heads all the way round the middle of the foam ball, working from top to bottom. Then glue on a second line of rose heads around the middle of the ball at right angles to the first, so dividing the ball into four quarter sections, like a traditional pomander.

3 Fill in the quarters with the remaining rose heads, then insert small pieces of eucalyptus between the flowers to hide any gaps.

4 Knot the ends of the ribbon to make a handle of the correct length, and finish off with a large bow.

TULIP POMANDER

Instead of exotic aromas, this beautiful fresh pomander is rich in contrasting textures: the spiky inner petals of double tulips, beady black myrtle berries and soft grey moss are all set against smooth satin ribbon.

- 13 cm (5 in) diameter florist's foam ball
- 2 m (2 yd) satin ribbon
- scissors
- 20 heads 'Appleblossom'
- double tulips
- myrtle stems
- stub (floral) wires
- wire cutters
- reindeer moss

1 Soak the foam ball in water. Tie the ribbon around the ball, starting at the top and crossing it over at the bottom, then tying at the top to divide the ball into four equal segments.

2 Cut the tulip stems to 2.5 cm (1 in) and push them carefully into the foam. Arrange five tulips in a vertical line down the centre of each segment.

3 Cut sprigs of myrtle on short stems and push them into the foam to form lines on either side of each line of tulips. The myrtle should appear quite compact.

4 Form short staples from sections of stub (floral) wire and use them to secure pieces of reindeer moss between the flowers to cover any remaining exposed areas of the foam ball.

TOPIARY TREES

The satisfying precision of smoothly clipped box or yew topiary is fun to reproduce using dried flowers or foliage, and this is an effective way to show dried flowers at their best.  The scent and beauty of the flowerheads are concentrated in the tightly controlled arrangement, while the decoration is given structure and height by mounting it on a trunk or stem in an elegant container.

 As alternatives to symmetrical, mop-head trees sitting squarely in their pots, you can use contorted, twisted stems or tree roots for designs with an oriental character, resembling ancient bonsai.

MOP-HEAD LAVENDER TREE

Make a pair of these enchanting lavender trees, then position them on either side of a mantelpiece mirror or fireplace in a witty allusion to real mop-head bay trees growing on either side of a front door.

- sharp knife
- 2 x 20 cm (8 in) diameter florist's dry foam balls
- 20 cm (8 in) diameter container
- 1 m (40 in) piece

- contorted willow
- dried lavender stems
- scissors
- stub (floral) wires
- wire cutters
- reindeer moss

1 Using the knife, cut one of the florist's foam balls in half and place in the container with one cut side uppermost. Use extra foam if necessary to fill the container. Insert two 50 cm (20 in) lengths of contorted willow stem into the foam.

2 Attach the other foam ball to the top of the willow stems. Choose stems of lavender which have heads of similar sizes and trim the stems to 2.5 cm (1 in). Make a ring of lavender around the ball, then make a second ring at right angles to it.

3 Fill in each section of the foam ball with lavender heads, working in rows to achieve an even finished result.

4 Bend short lengths of stub (floral) wire into staples and use them to pin the reindeer moss over the foam in the pot.

COPPER BEECH TOPIARY TREE

The exuberant flowers and foliage in this design spill over the edge of the container as well as forming the mop-head top of the tree. Miniature terracotta pots add to its textural interest.

- large terracotta flowerpot
- self-hardening clay
- 45 cm (18 in) length of rustic pole
- 13 cm (5 in) diameter florist's dry foam ball
- small pieces of florist's dry foam
- 2 large bunches glycerined copper beech foliage
- scissors
- stub (floral) wires
- 12 miniature terracotta flowerpots
- 2 bunches dried solidago
- florist's reel wire
- glue gun, if needed
- 2 bunches poppy heads

1 Half fill the large terracotta pot with self-hardening clay. Stand the length of rustic pole centrally in the pot, pushing it down into the clay. Leave until the clay is completely hard.

2 Press the florist's foam ball on to the top of the trunk, making sure it is firmly in place but not pressing it so far down that the trunk comes out of the top of the ball. Cover the base with pieces of florist's dry foam.

3 Cover the ball and the foam in the base with sprigs of copper beech or other preserved foliage. Thread stub (floral) wires through the holes in the miniature flowerpots and twist to make a stem with which to attach them to the tree and the base.

4 Arrange the pots throughout the tree and the base, and fill with small wired bunches of solidago, trimming them with scissors where needed. These can be glued into position if necessary, using the glue gun. Finally, add the poppy heads throughout the tree and base.

EUCALYPTUS TREE

Preserved eucalyptus leaves have a strong perfume when new which fades a little after a while, but this tree will last a very long time. Trim the sprigs of eucalyptus as close to the leaves as you can, to make sure that no bare stems are visible in the display. For a fuller appearance, wire small bunches of leaves together and push them in between the stems.

- terracotta flowerpot
- self-hardening clay
- 38 cm (15 in) length of rustic pole
- 15 cm (6 in) florist's dry foam ball
- reindeer moss
- mossing (floral) pins or glue gun
- 8–10 bunches *Eucalyptus spiralus*
- scissors

1 Half fill the terracotta flowerpot with self-hardening clay. Stand the pole centrally in the pot and push the foam ball firmly on to the top. Fix reindeer moss into the top of the pot using mossing (floral) pins, or a glue gun if the clay is already hard. Leave the base to harden completely.

2 Cut all the eucalyptus into sprigs about 10 cm (4 in) long, trimming away the lowest leaves so that 2.5 cm (1 in) of stem can be pushed into the foam. Push them, one at a time, into the foam ball, keeping hold of the opposite side of the ball so that you don't push it off the top of the trunk.

3 Go on adding the stems until the whole ball is covered. Remember to stand back from the display frequently so that you can check that you have added the stems evenly and kept the spherical shape.

MARJORAM AND BAY TREE

Oregano will keep its colour for a very long time, so it's ideal for a dried arrangement in a bright location. If you have access to fresh stems of bay, add them straight from the bush and they will slowly dry out in the display.

- terracotta flowerpot
- self-hardening clay
- 38 cm (15 in) length of rustic pole
- reindeer moss
- mossing (floral) pins
- glue gun
- 15 cm (6 in) diameter florist's dry foam ball
- 8–10 bunches marjoram
- stub (floral) wires
- wire cutters
- bay stems
- sharp knife
- oregano
- twig bundles

1 Fill the bottom of the terracotta pot with clay and set the rustic pole centrally in it. Fix the moss into the top of the pot using the mossing (floral) pins, or a glue gun if the clay is already hard. Leave the base to harden completely. When the base is dry, lift it out, glue it and replace it in the pot. Push the foam ball on to the top of the trunk.

2 Wire all the marjoram in small bunches no more than 10 cm (4 in) in length. Push the bunches one at a time into the foam, always supporting the opposite side of the ball so that you don't push it off the top of the trunk. Stand back from the display as you work, to check that you have added all the bunches evenly and kept the spherical shape.

3 Continue to add bunches of marjoram until the whole of the foam ball has been covered. Cut the bay stems vertically to separate sprays of one or two leaves. Wire them in bunches or individually. Bunch the oregano with stub (floral) wires.

4 Turn the whole tree upside-down and push the bay stems and oregano into the foam, all around the top of the trunk. There should be no bay stems showing. Twist wires round the centres of the twig bundles and distribute them throughout the arrangement.

Keep all the bunches as even as possible, and the same length. This helps when putting the tree together, and will ensure that you achieve a perfect sphere. When the display has started to look a little tired, it can be sprayed with florist's clear lacquer to bring back some of the colour of the bay and the other herbs.

TULIP TOPIARY TREE

Choose large double tulips to make this impressive decoration. Their layers of different-sized petals combine to create a very dense, rounded head for the tree, like a huge peony.

- florist's dry foam block
- sharp knife
- basket
- raffia
- 5 x 30 cm (12 in) cinnamon sticks
- scissors
- glue gun

- sand or stones if needed
- stub (floral) wires
- reindeer moss
- 15 cm (6 in) diameter florist's foam ball
- 30 double tulips

1 Trim the dry foam block so that it fits into the basket. Using raffia, tie the cinnamon sticks together at both top and bottom and push the bundle about 4 cm (1½ in) into the foam, securing it with glue.

2 If necessary, stabilize the basket with sand or stones under the foam. Bend stub (floral) wires into staples and use these to pin reindeer moss over the dry foam block, completely covering the base of the tree.

3 Soak the florist's foam ball in water. Carefully apply a small amount of glue to the top of the cinnamon stick trunk and then push the wet foam ball approximately 4 cm (1½ in) down on to it.

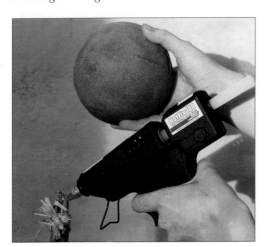

4 Make sure that the tulip heads are as open as possible by holding each flower in your hand and gently spreading the petals back, even to the extent of folding the outermost petals inside-out.

5 Cut the tulip stems to a length of approximately 4 cm (1½ in) and push them into the soaked foam ball, covering the surface evenly. Handle the flowerheads carefully to avoid crushing them.

ORNAMENTAL CABBAGE TREE

Decorative trees can be created from all sorts of materials. This unusual design uses ornamental cabbage heads to form the foliage crown of the tree, set on a twisted stem reminiscent of bonsai. With regular misting, the arrangement will keep fresh for a week or more.

- medium-sized terracotta pot
- cellophane (plastic wrap)
- sand
- florist's dry foam block
- sharp knife
- piece of dried tree root

- 2 large handfuls soaked sphagnum moss
- garden twine
- scissors
- stub (floral) wires
- 10 miniature ornamental cabbages

1 Line the pot with cellophane (plastic wrap) and half fill it with sand. Cut a piece of florist's dry foam and wedge it into the pot.

2 Push the tree root into the foam block. Form a handful of sphagnum moss into a ball by criss-crossing it with garden twine.

4 Using stub (floral) wires, wire the ornamental cabbages individually, twisting the projecting ends together. Stitch-wire any loose cabbage leaves individually.

3 Push the moss ball on to the top of the root. Thread stub (floral) wires horizontally through it, pull down the ends and wrap them around the root to secure the moss.

5 Push the projecting wires into the moss ball to cover it completely and evenly with the cabbage heads. Fill any remaining gaps with the individual leaves.

6 Bend stub (floral) wires into staples with which to fix the sphagnum moss to the dry foam at the base of the tree, making sure that it hides the dry foam completely.

APPLE AND LAVENDER TREE

This unusual tree has two twisted trunks and therefore needs a very stable base. The flowers and fruit have been chosen for their soft colours: pale green phalaris and Nigella orientalis, dusty blue lavender, soft grey eucalyptus and creamy roses and apples.

- 15 cm (6 in) terracotta pot
- cellophane (plastic wrap)
- sand
- sharp knife
- florist's dry foam block
- glue gun
- dried tree root with two branches
- 2 x 12 cm (4¾ in) florist's dry foam balls
- 60 dried apple slices
- stub (floral) wires
- 150 stems natural phalaris
- scissors
- wire cutters
- 30 stems dried cream roses
- 50 stems *Nigella orientalis*
- 20 stems ti tree
- 150 stems dried lavender
- 12 short stems dried eucalyptus

1 Line the terracotta pot with cellophane (plastic wrap) and three-quarters fill it with wet sand. Trim the florist's dry foam block to fit the pot. Wedge it firmly in on top of the sand and level it with the rim of the pot.

2 Put a little glue on the base of the piece of root and push it into the centre of the dry foam block. Apply some glue to the top of the branches and push a florist's dry foam ball on to each branch.

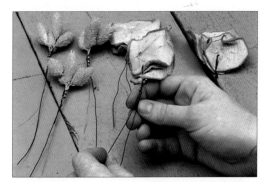

3 Using stub (floral) wires, wire the apple slices in groups of three, twisting the ends together. Cut the phalaris stems to about 3 cm (1¼ in) and wire them in 30 groups of five.

4 Trim the wires of the phalaris bunches to 4 cm (1½ in) and distribute them evenly, all over the two foam balls. Cut the stems of the dried roses to 5 cm (2 in) and push them into the foam, distributing them evenly among the phalaris.

5 Trim the wires of the apple slices to 4 cm (1½ in) and push them into the foam balls. Cut 40 stems of *Nigella orientalis* and the ti tree stems to 5 cm (2 in) and add them to the arrangement, distributing them evenly.

6 Cut the lavender stems to an overall length of 5 cm (2 in), form them into 40 groups of three and push the stems of each group into the foam throughout the arrangement to give an interesting spiky effect.

7 Cut the eucalyptus stems and the remaining *Nigella orientalis* and lavender stems to varying lengths. Push these into the florist's foam at the base of the tree to cover the foam completely.

OREGANO TOPIARY TREE

Oregano retains both its colour and its scent for a long time so it is an ideal herb to choose for a large project such as this tree. If you make sure that every bunch of the herb is trimmed to the same size you should have no difficulty in making a perfect sphere.

- 15 cm (6 in) diameter terracotta pot
- self-hardening clay
- 38 cm (15 in) length of rustic pole
- reindeer moss
- mossing (floral) pins
- glue gun
- 15 cm (6 in) diameter florist's dry foam ball
- 8–10 bunches oregano
- scissors
- stub (floral) wires
- wire cutters

1 Fill the bottom of the terracotta pot with clay and set the rustic pole centrally in it. Fix the moss into the top of the pot using the mossing (floral) pins, or use a glue gun if the clay is already hard. Leave the base to harden. When the base is dry, lift it out, glue it and replace it in the pot.

2 Push the foam ball on to the top of the trunk. Trim, bunch and wire all the oregano, keeping each bunch to no more than 10 cm (4 in) in length. Push the bunches into the ball, supporting the opposite side. To avoid crushing the leaves, hold each bunch as far down the stem as possible.

3 Continue adding bunches until the whole ball is covered and there are no spaces. Use mossing (floral) pins to cover the foam around the trunk with moss, in case the tree is set high up where the underside will be visible.

ROSE TOPIARY TREE

Without doubt, roses are among the most extravagant of flowers. In the same way that the powerful scent of a fresh rose can unexpectedly halt a passer-by, so dried roses can make arresting topiary designs. Combine contrasting colours for dramatic effect or experiment with muted pastel shades for a more subtle look.

- 10–12 bunches dried roses
- scissors
- stub (floral) wires
- small-headed flowers such as *Achillea* 'Lilac Beauty', *Achillea ptarmica* 'The Pearl', *Alchemilla mollis*, bupleurum, marjoram, oregano, solidago
- prepared potted trunk with mossed base and foam ball attached

1 Steam the roses to open the petals and increase the size of the flowerheads. Trim the stems to 7.5–10 cm (3–4 in), depending on how large you want the finished tree to be.

2 Wire small bunches of 3–4 flowers together, leaving the leaves attached to the stems. Trim and wire the leaves from the waste stems to provide extra greenery for the tree.

3 Push the wired bunches of flowers, one at a time, into the foam ball, keeping the design even. Fill in the remaining spaces with small flowers, always supporting the foam ball with your hand on the opposite side to where you are working.

DOUBLE ROSE TREE

*This little double-headed rose tree makes a break with convention.
'Yellow Dot' commercially grown spray roses open fully to a
pretty rosette shape. The same design could be made using dried
rosebuds, but you would need considerably more flowers.
Kept cool and frequently misted, this fresh rose tree should last
for at least a week.*

- 2 balls and 1 block florist's foam
- sharp knife
- medium-sized terracotta pot
- 3 bamboo canes,
  45 cm (18 in) long
- thick pliable string
- scissors
- 10 stems leucadendron
- 10 stems spray roses
- 1 handful sphagnum moss

1 Soak the florist's foam
thoroughly. Cut a piece of the
block to fit tightly into the pot.
Insert the bamboo canes together
and carefully position the foam
balls centrally on the canes. Bind
the string around the canes and
tie the ends securely.

2 Cut off the leucadendron heads,
leaving about 2 cm (¾ in) of stem,
and insert into the foam balls at
regular intervals. Insert the roses
in the same way. Cover the
surface of the pot with the
sphagnum moss to conceal the
foam completely.

FIR CONE TREE

You should be able to find most of the materials for this inexpensive tree in your local woods. The most costly element is your time, as working with fir cones can be quite fiddly. Spray the finished tree with a little clear lacquer to give the cones a fresh sheen.

- terracotta pot
- self-hardening clay
- 38 cm (15 in) rustic pole or bundle of straight twigs
- reindeer moss
- mossing (floral) pins

- fir cones
- stub (floral) wires or glue gun
- wire cutters
- 13 cm (5 in) diameter florist's dry foam ball

1 Fill the bottom of the terracotta pot with clay and set the tree trunk centrally in it. Fix the moss into the top of the pot using the mossing (floral) pins. Leave the base to harden completely. If you do not have a glue gun, wire each fir cone by looping a stub (floral) wire around it as close to the base as possible.

2 Secure the wire by bending the two ends down and twisting them together. Trim the ends to a length of approximately 5 cm (2 in). Gently push the florist's dry foam ball on to the top of the tree trunk, adding a little glue if necessary to secure it. Reinforce the foam ball by wrapping some wire around it.

3 Add the wired fir cones to the tree, pushing them into the foam from the bottom upwards. Add hanks of moss firmly secured with mossing (floral) pins to fill any gaps. If you are using a glue gun, there is no need to wire the cones. Allow the hot glue to cool a little before attaching them so that the foam does not melt.

LONG-LASTING TOPIARY TREES

*Large topiary trees take a lot of dried plant material to produce
their lavish heads of flowers or foliage, and they make substantial
decorations which you will want to go on looking their best as long
as possible. Cones, seedheads and sturdy dried flowers make the
most durable trees, but you can also help to prolong the life of more
fragile flowers. Keep them dusted by playing a hairdryer, on a
cold setting, over the surface, and spray them with clear florist's
lacquer to revive fading colours. Most dried flowers will keep their
colours longer if they are protected from bright sunlight. Use the
techniques shown in the previous projects to create these variations.*

ROSE TREE

This delicate tree includes a small rose called 'Lilac Beauty', whose
petals fade to a rich cream colour. Oregano is interspersed among the
petals. The picture below shows the colours when the tree is newly
made, the picture on the right shows the roses faded to cream.

PAINTED ROSE TREE

When the flowers have faded and your large rose topiary is looking past its best, give it a new lease of life by spraying the whole tree – including the pot – with a fine coating of white paint. This technique can be applied to most old displays that you do not want to part with. Keep the paint can moving while you spray to distribute the paint evenly. Other colours can be used equally well, but if you choose gold for a festive effect, apply a base coat of white paint first, to stop the original colours of the flowers and pot from dulling the golden shine. Add a few fir cones to the arrangement to complete the wintry effect.

POPPY SEEDHEADS

These magnificent grey poppy seedheads need no special treatment in order to last for many years. Resist the temptation to spray them with lacquer as this will rob them of their subtle grey-white bloom. Depending on the strength and length of their stems, you may need to support them with stub (floral) wires before arranging them. Cover the foam ball with reindeer moss before adding the poppy heads to hide any gaps. Extra twigs planted around the central trunk prevent this design from looking top-heavy.

PROTEAS

Topiary designs made with durable materials like protea provide a dramatic alternative to more everyday flower mixtures. They are also ideal for a first attempt at topiary because the material is so sturdy that it is quite difficult to make a mistake. Cover the foam ball with a good layer of moss to prevent any foam showing between the proteas. This tree has the advantage of an extremely long life, and needs only an occasional dusting to keep it looking its best for a long time.

DESIGNING WITH LEAVES

Foliage is often used only as a filler in floral designs, but it can make striking and unusual arrangements when used alone. Preserved leaves are much easier to work with than foliage that has simply been left to dry naturally. Copper beech and oak are easiest to find, but from a good supplier you should be able to obtain box, bughina, eucalyptus, hoya, leather leaf fern, poplar and other species. If the foliage is wrapped in plastic when you buy it, hang it up for a few days in a warm, dry place, to give any residual preservative time to evaporate. On the other hand, if it is very dry, wrap it loosely in paper and hang it upside-down in the steamy atmosphere of the kitchen.

OAK LEAF CONES

These impressive trees will add interest to a garden or conservatory throughout the year, and are simple to make. Set a trunk in a plastic pot filled with self-hardening clay and fix a florist's dry foam cone to the trunk. Wind florist's reel wire 2–3 times around the pot to secure it, then wind it from the bottom of the pot upwards, holding reindeer moss firmly in place as you do so to cover the pot completely. Cover the foam cone with small wired bunches of 6–8 preserved oak leaves pushed in at random to allow the leaves to fan out. Use smaller bunches to fill any gaps.

RAFFIA-BOUND TREES

A stunning pair of stylized trees can be made using only limited materials. The design on the left uses preserved poplar leaves, pinned into a florist's dry foam cone using mossing (floral) pins. The other tree is made in the same way using bughina leaves, and decorated with a bundle of lavender and cinnamon sticks. The key to success is to overlap the leaves so that they hide the pins. Use a glue gun as well as pins if you wish. The raffia bows look as though they are holding the leaves in place, but in this instance they are purely decorative.

FERN TREES

These trees made using preserved ferns are full of movement and life and have a natural, windswept look. Prepare each pot by half filling it with self-hardening clay and setting a trunk in the centre. Pin reindeer moss in place using mossing (floral) pins and leave the clay to harden. Fix a florist's dry foam cone or ball to the top of the trunk and pin a rough layer of moss over it – this does not have to look perfect as most of the moss will be hidden. Wire the stems of the ferns using stub (floral) wires. Give the arrangement as much movement as you can by adding the ferns at angles, so that they look as if they flow into each other, rather than aiming for a smooth topiary effect.

BLUE SPRUCE TREE

Blue spruce always looks luxurious and also has a wonderful pungent smell when fresh. This blue spruce tree design makes a perfect winter display and can be embellished with festive details for Christmas, whether you make a small tree (as shown in the steps) or a larger version to provide a welcome by the front door.

- terracotta pot
- self-hardening clay
- 38 cm (15 in) length of rustic pole or twig bundle
- reindeer moss
- mossing (floral) pins
- 15 cm (6 in) diameter florist's dry foam ball
- blue spruce
- scissors
- dried roses
- stub (floral) wires
- wire cutters
- fir cones
- walnuts
- chestnuts
- pencil
- glue gun or all-purpose glue
- small twig bundle
- raffia or ribbon

1 Fill the bottom of the terracotta pot with clay and set the pole or twig bundle centrally in it. Fix the moss into the top of the pot using mossing (floral) pins. Leave the base to harden completely. Fix the foam ball to the top of the trunk. Cut the blue spruce into lengths of about 15 cm (6 in), trimming away the needles to expose about 2.5 cm (1 in) of stem to push into the foam. Cover the ball completely and evenly with the blue spruce.

2 Wire the dried roses into small bunches of 3–4 flowers using stub (floral) wires. Add them to the tree at random, well spaced out. Wire the fir cones around their bases and add them, keeping the arrangement balanced.

3 Wire the walnuts and chestnuts: curl the end of a wire around a pencil, then glue this circle of wire to each nut. When all the other materials are in place, add a wired bundle of twigs tied with raffia or ribbon in a lavish bow.

SEASHELL TREE

*A tree made of seashells will last forever, and needs only an occasional dusting to keep it clean. It makes an unusual decoration
for a bathroom, where the atmosphere would be too damp for arrangements of dried flowers.*

- terracotta pot
- self-hardening clay
- 38 cm (15 in) twig
  bundle
- reindeer moss
- mossing (floral)
- pins
- 15 cm (6 in)
  diameter florist's
  dry foam ball
- shells
- glue gun

1 Fill the bottom of the terracotta pot with
clay and set the twig bundle for the trunk
centrally in it. Fix the moss into the top of the
pot using mossing (floral) pins. Leave the base
to harden completely. Fix the foam ball to the
top of the trunk.

2 Using the glue gun, attach the shells firmly
to the foam ball to cover it completely, filling
in any small gaps with moss. Alternatively, you
may prefer to glue on the shells before
mounting the foam ball, leaving a hole for
the trunk. Once the ball is in position, fill in
any gaps around the trunk with more shells
and moss.

CONES AND OBELISKS

Conical arrangements follow the natural shape of many trees, and always look elegant in classic terracotta pots, as they also reflect the shape of the pot. They are particularly appropriate at Christmas, when they can be decorated to resemble miniature Christmas trees, but these arrangements will go on looking good for many months. Cones and obelisks are splendidly evocative of

the gardening and architectural styles of the 17th century. It's well worth making a pair to do full justice to their symmetry and restrained use of colour and form.

FLOWER CONE

This unusual design features a series of stacked rings, each composed of one type and colour of flower, to create a strong geometric pattern. One side of the metal container is higher than the other, and this is exploited by making the rings of flowers follow this elliptical shape to sweep down from back to front.

- 28 cm (11 in) florist's dry foam cone
- 11 cm (4½ in) diameter galvanized metal container
- scissors
- 20 stems dried floss flowers
- 40 stems dried pink roses
- 20 stems dried marjoram
- 10 stems small dried globe thistles
- ribbon

1 Wedge the dry foam cone firmly into the metal container. Cut the floss flower stems to about 2.5 cm (1 in) and arrange them in a ring, following the rim of the container. Cut the rose stems to about 2.5 cm (1 in) and, immediately above the first ring, arrange a second ring of rose heads.

2 Cut the stems of the marjoram and globe thistles to about 2.5 cm (1 in). Immediately above the roses, make a third ring with the marjoram and then a fourth with the thistles. Repeat the sequence of rings until the whole of the cone is covered. At the top, fix a single rose.

3 Wrap the ribbon around the metal container and finish it in a small bow tied at the front.

CHRISTMAS CONE

This delightful little tree, made from dyed, preserved oak leaves and decorated with tiny gilded cones, would make an enchanting Christmas decoration, either singly or as one of a group forming a table centrepiece.

- sharp knife
- bunch of dyed, preserved oak leaves
- florist's reel wire
- stub (floral) wires
- small fir cones
- picture framer's wax gilt
- small florist's dry foam cone
- 18 cm (7 in) terracotta pot
- 18 cm (7 in) florist's dry foam cone

1 Cut the oak leaves off the branches and trim the stems. Wire bunches of about four leaves, making some bunches with small leaves, some with medium-sized and others with large leaves. Sort the bunches into piles.

2 Bend pieces of stub (floral) wire in half, then wind around each fir cone, as near the base as possible, and twist the ends together. Gild each cone by rubbing on picture framer's wax gilt with your fingers.

3 Cut the smaller foam cone to fit the pot and wedge it in. Push in stub (floral) wires to attach the larger cone. Attach the bunches of leaves to the cone, starting at the top with the small leaves and using larger leaves as you work down, to make a realistic shape. Finish by adding the gilded cones.

SPICE TOPIARY CONE

Fashion a delightfully aromatic, culinary topiary from cloves and star anise, pot it in terracotta decorated with cinnamon sticks and top it with a cinnamon-stick cross. Sticking all the cloves into the florist's foam is both easy and therapeutic.

- small "long Tom" terracotta pot
- sharp knife
- cinnamon sticks
- glue gun
- 23 cm (9 in) florist's dry foam cone
- small florist's dry foam cone
- stub (floral) wires
- star anise
- wire cutters
- cloves

1 Prepare the terracotta pot by cutting the cinnamon sticks with a sharp knife to the length of the pot and gluing them in position, evenly spaced, around the side.

2 Trim the top of the larger foam cone. Cut the smaller cone to fit inside the pot. Push four stub (floral) wires into the pot and position the larger cone over them.

3 Sort out about 20 complete star anise. Pass two wires over the front of each star anise in a cross and twist the ends together at the back. Trim the wires to 1 cm (½ in).

4 Arrange the star anise in rows of three down the cone to quarter it. Add two more in the centre of each quarter. Fill the remaining area of the cone with cloves, packing them tightly so that none of the foam shows through.

5 Glue two short pieces of cinnamon stick into a cross. Wire it and use to decorate the top of the cone.

LAVENDER OBELISK

Evoke the sumptuous style of the 17th century with a magnificent beribboned obelisk. It is very easy to make and the result is fabulous. However, if you don't have a lavender hedge that you can plunder, it could be a fairly costly project, so scale it down if you prefer.

- sharp knife
- 50 cm (20 in) dry florist's foam cone
- 30 cm (12 in) diameter metal urn
- dressmaker's pins
- 2m (2¼ yd) wire-edged ribbon,
- 5 cm (2 in) wide
- 12 dried poppy seedheads
- 10 large bunches of lavender

1 Using a knife, score a circle around the diameter of the cone about 7.5 cm (3 in) up from the bottom, then carefully carve back the base to fit the shape of the urn.

2 Try the cone in the urn. If it does not yet fit, carve away a little more of the foam. Keep trying the cone to see if it fits and trim the foam until it does.

3 Using pins, fix the wire-edged ribbon to the cone: start at the bottom and work around to the top, then work back down again to make a trellis effect. Scrunch the ribbon slightly as you go to give a fuller effect.

4 Position one poppy seedhead at the top of the cone, and the others at intervals around it. Cut the lavender stems to 2.5 cm (1 in) and fix a ring of lavender all around the base of the obelisk where it meets the urn.

5 Working in rows, gradually fill in each section within the ribbons. As you reach a poppy seedhead, take it out so that you can place lavender near the hole, then replace it.

PYRAMID FIR CONE POT

This conical arrangement is simply built up using moss and fir cones, with no underlying florist's foam cone, though you could use one if you prefer. It makes a perfect winter decoration. You may wish to spray it lightly with white paint to give a delicate frosted effect.

- terracotta pot
- florist's dry foam block
- sharp knife
- glue gun
- reindeer moss
- fir cones

1 Fill the terracotta pot with florist's dry foam, wedged in tightly. Make sure that the exposed top is level, as this is the base of the pyramid of cones. Glue a layer of reindeer moss around the top edge of the pot.

2 Glue on the first layer of cones around the rim of the pot. When this is complete, add the next layer, laying the cones in slightly overlapping circles to build up the shape. Glue on the cones horizontally, pointing outwards. Go on building in circles until the arrangement is complete. Fill in any gaps with moss.

OAK LEAF CONE

This striking preserved oak leaf sculpture is extremely time-consuming to construct, but although the method is fiddly, it is quite straightforward. Using a foam cone, pin each preserved oak leaf in place with a mossing pin, working from the top downwards. Then position the next leaf to hide the previous pin. Alternatively, fix the leaves in place with glue. The sculpture makes an interesting, unexpected focal point. If you have the patience to make two, use a foam ball to make a sphere and place it beside the cone for maximum impact.

HERB OBELISK

A colourful pillar of herbs and vegetables looks wonderful on its own and even more striking when it is one of a pair.
It is particularly suitable as a buffet table decoration, but would look lovely almost anywhere.

- ruler
- pencil
- florist's foam block
- sharp knife
- urn
- 7 radishes
- 8 button mushrooms
- 9 small, clean new potatoes

- stub (floral) wires
- scissors
- dill
- curry plant
- marjoram
- mint
- bay leaves

1 Using a ruler and pencil, score the cutting lines for the obelisk on the florist's dry foam block. Carve the block to the required shape with a sharp knife. Soak the carved foam shape and secure firmly in the urn.

2 Wire each of the vegetables by carefully pushing a stub (floral) wire through the base and twisting the ends together. Arrange them in horizontal rings around the obelisk, working up from the bottom.

3 Fill in the gaps between the rings of vegetables, using a different herb for each ring. Select a quantity of bay leaves and insert them into the florist's foam under the bottom layer of vegetables to create a formal border.

GILDED FIG PYRAMID

An almost profligate use of figs produces a gloriously decadent decoration for the festive table. The deep purple figs with their dusting of gold, arranged with geometric precision, create an opulent yet architectural focal point for the most indulgent Christmas feasts.

- 25 cm (10 in) florist's dry foam cone
- gilded terracotta flowerpot
- all-purpose glue

- 40 black figs
- picture framer's wax gilt
- stub (floral) wires
- 50 ivy leaves

1 Make sure that the dry foam cone sits comfortably in the pot. To ensure that it is stable, put a drop of glue around the edge of the cone base. Gild the figs slightly on one side of the fruit only, by rubbing the wax gilt on to the skin with your fingers.

2 Wire the gilded figs by pushing a stub (floral) wire horizontally through the flesh approximately 2.5 cm (1 in) above the base of the fruit. Carefully bend the two protruding pieces of wire so that they point downwards. Take care not to tear the skin of the figs.

3 Attach the figs to the cone by pushing their wires into the foam. Work in concentric circles around the cone, moving up from the bottom.

*W*hen you are buying the fresh figs, choose the firmest fruit available as they will damage less easily and keep for longer.

4 When you reach the top, position the last fig on the tip of the dry foam cone, with its stem pointing upwards to create a point.

5 Make hairpin shapes out of stub (floral) wires and fix the ivy leaves into the cone between the figs, covering any exposed foam.

Index